THE PRICE OF EVERYTHING

Andrew Motion was born in 1952 and educated at
University College, Oxford. He is the author of six previous
books of poems, of two biographies, including the
authorized life of Philip Larkin, and of critical studies of
Larkin and Edward Thomas, and he has been the recipient
of the John Llewellyn Rhys Prize, the Somerset Maugham
Award, the Dylan Thomas Award and the Whitbread Prize
for Biography. He lives in London with his wife and their
three children.

The Price of Everything

ANDREW MOTION

faber and faber
LONDON BOSTON

First published in 1994
by Faber and Faber Limited
3 Queen Square London WC1N 3AU

Phototypeset by Wilmaset Ltd, Wirral
Printed in England by Clays Ltd, St Ives plc

© Andrew Motion, 1994

Andrew Motion is hereby identified
as the author of this work in accordance with
Section 77 of the Copyright, Designs
and Patents Act 1988.

A CIP record for this book
is available from the British Library

ISBN 0–571–16900–7

10 9 8 7 6 5 4 3 2 1

For Jan Dalley

Contents

A Note and Acknowledgements

Both the poems in this book are about various kinds of conflict, and both take the First World War as their starting point. *Lines of Desire* was written over several years, each of its parts emerging unpredictably. *Joe Soap* was written more quickly, and has a more obvious narrative structure.

I gratefully acknowledge the following: Elizabeth and Mervyn Dalley, Alan Hollinghurst, Blake Morrison; the *Guardian*, the *Independent*, the *Independent on Sunday*, the *London Review of Books*, the *Times Literary Supplement*; *Rupert Brooke: A Biography* by Christopher Hassall (Faber, 1964), *Wilfred Owen: The Last Year* by Dominic Hibberd (Constable, 1992), *A Paper House: The Ending of Yugoslavia* by Mark Thompson (Vintage, 1992), *Memorial Candles: Children of the Holocaust* by Dina Wardi (Tavistock/Routledge, 1992); and *In the Name of God: The Khomeni Decade* by Robin Wright (Bloomsbury, 1990).

LINES OF DESIRE

Dedication

In broad daylight and a familiar street –
the sort where gossips dawdle and nose-to-tail dogs meet –

some bastard with no face lurched out from behind a tree
and tried to kill me.

There was tooth-flash, black leather, the smile of a knife
and I saw the terrified puffed-out bird of my life

fly from my hand – so for a long second I knew I was dead
even though I was still fighting him off, even though I'd just
                                                      said

No! No! and then in a flurried muddle *Go on! Go on!*
(meaning all I most wanted to do in the world had hardly
                                                      begun)

before my heart started working again and I stood there alone
dribbling a little thin blood from one finger on to a ringing
                                                      paving-stone.

*

I thought that was it
but then night fell

and the knife became
an adder's tongue

bitterly licking me,
slicing easily,

stripping the brain
from my open head

until all I'd begun,
half-finished, done,

or wished to be true
was gone. All except you.

*

But you were asleep and made no sound
when I left your side without a word

and slipped downstairs to my room underground,
a grown man like a frightened child.

The fire is out at the heart of the world;
all tame creatures have grown up wild.

The lives I trusted, even my own,
collapse, break off, or don't belong.

I leant my head on the window pane
and the hard-edged garden, lit with rain,

shimmered a million knives; the wind
caressed them with its painful hand.

The fire is out at the heart of the world;
all tame creatures have grown up wild —

all except you, your life like a cloud
I am lost in now and will never be found.

1 A Dream of Peace

It starts like this
with stick or stone
or sharpened bone

and a hill in the wilds
where a crotchety oak
soughs over a cave

and the face of fire
flares all day
all night all day

and *clink clinkety clink*
might be the hammer
of something new

or might be a bird
buried deep in the oak
which sings its heart out

with nothing to say
except what happens
to strike home next.

*

It starts like that and it comes to this:
my father's tank – *clank clankety clank* –
just one of hundreds, sprigged with leaves,
on a rippling road through northern France,

and blossoming light on apple trees,
and singing larks like dots in the sun,
and easy climbs and the summer wind,
and the . . .

*

In a twinkling the sun has vanished behind a barn, then it is out
again. A moment ago he would have sworn everything looked
like home – like Essex! But when he turns off the road into a
field it is not like Essex at all. On the bank of a stream is a
soldier's fair-haired head with no jaw to it, no mouth. This is
all he can find.

*

I wanted a big language for the people who died –
I wanted a big language for fighting. I found one,
but only when peace descended; then I looked back
and the apple-roads, my vanished brothers-in-arms,
the ruined flickering outskirts of the capital,
a dead dog in a pram, the enormous iron station
with its roof blown off, the herded people
all were part of my big language.
                              I filled my lungs
and shouted until I had ripped the leaves from every tree in
                                                        sight
and raised a creamy wave on even the smallest buried lakes.
My language had conquered the world.
I was free to say what I wanted.

*

When I was a boy at the head of the stairs
my life was the life of the senses.
I cooled my face at a window above the yard

and saw in the melting distance a second boy
who could have been just like me but was not,
flapping his arms like someone about to take off

if only he could get free of the tangling grass
and the dull weight of his shoes, and the geese
he was driving ahead in a brilliant scattering cloud.

The grass, the wet, the melting light, the geese.
It was panicky, but it had something to do with peace.

*

What should I die for?
Answer me that.
What should I live for?
Clickety clack.

Give me your answer.
Clickety clack.
Show me a war
then take it back.

*

I fell in love with a soldier
seventy years younger than me,
who knew the country best
as soon as he left it to die.

Under a beech tree in Essex
he practised how it would go,
squeezing a gun barrel into his mouth
then deciding no.

But I knew nothing of that:
I only saw a soldier
hearing how death would be
in the dry crack of branches

echoing endlessly.

    *

I knew nothing, or less than nothing.
I knew books.
I knew
'Gas! Gas! Quick, boys!'
and learnt it,
saying it slowly:
'Gas! Gas! Quick, boys!'
The wrong war, the wrong speed, the wrong accent.

Nobody noticed.
In the dusty classroom
sunlight went solid with dust.
Quick! Quick!
Slow. Slow.
My tongue turned heavily over
and sank in the deepest sleep.
I knew nothing, or less than nothing.
The wrong war, the wrong speed, the wrong accent.

    *

Yes, I fell in love with a soldier
seventy years younger than me,
and after I had him by heart
I went to discover his grave.
This was not being brave.

Like mirrors, like snow, like chips of ice
white stones appear outside a wood.
Quick! Quick! It will soon be dark
and I won't be able to read their names
or come here again.

His voice ran by like a wave on a buried lake,
so quiet I had to hold my breath.
There it was then! A whisper and gone –
a secret I wanted to have as my own
if I ever got home.

*

I dreamed a woman made me take off my ring
(my father's ring) and at once I imagined a man
who stopped by a river somewhere up north from here
and threw in a ribbon which showed how brave he was.

Then in my dream the man was smothered by smoke
and I was aloft, catching the woman (the same woman)
up in my arms so we flew like a wounded gull,
me in my black, her in a rippling wedding-dress.

The whole country spread itself open below –
towns and villages, motorways, ring-roads, lanes,
water-logged moorland, grazing, a plain of wheat –
and we knew it contained whatever we meant by home.

The moon came out, and down we dipped close to the earth
where elm-tops tickled the woman's defenceless feet
and we searched for the intimate, beautiful detail in things:
a marbled starling, for instance, asleep on a telephone line.

By now I was tired and knew we had left it too late;
all we could see was wire, and too many eyes,
and a big gate like a grill wherever we went,
and a searchlight we could not escape for a moment longer.

We circled and circled, helplessly caught in each other,
not like a man and a woman at all, and not like a gull,
but a frivolous smidgin of paper blown up in a fire,
which twiddles away from the earth and cannot return.

*

What language to speak
in a world apart?
How to describe
peace in a heart?

My tongue woke up
but could not speak.
I opened my mouth:
clink clinkety clink.

*

They kept on jumping up, their happiness like a trampoline,
and set to at once. Chunks came away, rare as moonrock, or
fragments spiky with thick brown wire, or a whole door-
shaped section blurted over with writing. You couldn't read
what it said, no sentence came away complete, so what they
carried off were gasps and grunts.

   We slumped in our armchairs watching, my father and I,
and I wanted to know: did he recognize any of this? He shook
his head while I imagined the ruined flickering outskirts, the
enormous iron station with its roof blown off.

   'It must make you wonder?'

'Yup' was all he would say, 'Yup,' and kept on looking away.

*

Change the channel.

With our son between us
asleep and dreaming
the news floats up
in a blaring wash.

Press the button.

Now here is a soldier
who stands in the desert
and shouts a language
I do not know.

Change the channel.

Oh, but I see:
it's 'Gas! Gas! Gas!'
rattled so fast
it means nothing to me.

Press the button.

Now here is a tank
overtaken by camels –
it makes no sense.
Clank clankety clank.

Change the channel.

Oh, but I see:
the camels are leaving
the world where no one
expects to survive.

Press the button.

Now here is the nothing
we see in the dark
when pictures stop
and voices die.

Change the channel.

Oh, but I see:
it's not nothing at all —
two faces are there
in the creaking drizzle,

faint and silent,
while rising between them
the child wakes up
and cries to be fed.

Press the button.

    *

There's nothing special in this goodbye at my father's house:
too much to drink, too much to eat, too many rooms too
warm,

and the talk slowing down to traffic and the best and worst
way home
in a language not exactly dead but not exactly loving.

So let the music start. Then comes the spurt of tyres on gravel.
My father turns back to his house like someone walking
underwater.

2   Money Singing

It starts with the scream
of a porcupine saw
in a forester's yard.

It ends with the clunk
of walnut doors
in velvet halls.

It starts with the flash
of a furnace fire
under melting sand.

It ends with the chink
of crystal glasses
at priceless parties.

It starts with the clack
of a blurred shuttle
in furry air.

It ends with the sssh
of a satin slip
on a shaved leg.

*

There is mist rolling over the ground which is not mist and not
fog either, denser than both of them and darker, but when it
wraps itself round trees like mist or fog the birds stop singing
just as they do in mist or fog – a few forlorn cheeps then silence

and a lack of direction, the sense of happiness snuffed out for
ever.

No, it is not like mist or fog at all. It is a yellow gas-cloud
and the trees have no birds and no leaves or buds either, they
are skeletons, skeletons wringing their hands at the grotesque
moon-mess of mud they stand up in, and over which now,
wearing pig-masks and ant-eater noses, unexpectedly stumble
a line of soldiers. They would be shouting if there were anyone
alive to hear them shout; as it is they hiss, floundering under
the bare trees, working forward to where the air seems
brightest, the yellow mist or fog rolls away, then throwing
down their heavy rucksacks and weapons like men who no
longer care to know about defeat or victory or anything else,
tearing off their noses and pig-masks so we can see their very
own eyes are the wide bulging enormous things we thought
must have been glass, and charging down on us each with one
hand thrust forward to show the small coin we gave them
before any of this started.

*

Now here's a march that everyone knows
– *diddle de dumpty, dozhi doh* –
strap on your rucksack and tie up your shoes.

We're walking the country from north to south
– *diddle de dumpty, dozhi doh* –
so people can see what we say is the truth.

Cameras pop and our faces go
– *diddle de dumpty, dozhi doh* –
like leaves stripped from a sapling bough.

They fly in the air, they're no longer ours
– *diddle de dumpty, dozhi doh* –
and settle in crackling newspapers.

Now here they are on the classroom wall
– *diddle de dumpty, dozhi doh* –
a story which might not have happened at all.

*

I think I am about to lift my head,
my young head on young shoulders,
in the first classroom of my life.

I think I am about to step into these pictures,
alongside these marchers and goggle-eyed soldiers.
I think I am going to find out about money.

But the story breaks and I am left out.
Other soldiers appear, this time jammed in a boat
more like a tin trunk than a boat, which stops
on a white beach in France where the soldiers

spill out as if they were shy children arriving at a party.
This one, here, cannot stand it so sits down and cries:
he wants his mother. This one here is my father
and wants to change his trousers, to start off dry.

He wants to be neat and tidy if he is going to die.

He is thinking that if he lifts his head,
his young head on young shoulders,
he might see what any of this is worth.

He is thinking that somewhere over the sand dunes
in the solid world of roads and towns with civilians
he might discover someone to give him back what he has lost

if he can work out what that might be, and how much it cost.

*

Money is getting noisier.
He comes home at night
with figures jingling in his head.

Money is getting taller.
It whistles down at him
from new scaffolding in the old sites.

Money is getting long-faced.
It keeps his fingers busy
when he would rather be undoing a button.

Money is getting ambitious.
It wants him to sell his old banger
and sit a girl down beside him in comfort.

*

My mother and father
were Adam and Eve
back to the garden
hand in hand,
forgiven and blameless,
their lives their own.

But this was no garden:
this attic flat
was an eye on the Thames
blinded with rain,
their landlord's dog
a wolf at the door.

They didn't care;
for all they knew
love was the roof
above their heads,
love paid bills
and kept them fed.

By night they took
their deckled ledger
and counted the cost
of the life to come:
a child's clothes; a cot.

By day they wiped
their windows and saw
heavyweight, slow
dredgers explore
rich shipping-lanes below.

*

What does money feel like?
Tell me, tell me true:
Squelchy, greasy, slippy, wet;
that's what I tell you.

What does money feel like?
Tell me, since you know:
Burning, panting, rasping, dry;
that's what I tell you.

*

Softened-up, scrubbed, somewhere
between waking and sleeping
in the night-light dark
I become myself for the first time
when the bedroom door opens
and this ogre my father appears,
silent and drooping-shouldered
against the harsh passage light.

His one eye is a cigarette
reddening furiously as he steps
right up to me, bends close,
and leaks smoke into my hair;
there is a quick stir of bristles,
a saliva-smack, a half-grunt,
and I lie completely still
pressing one hand to my cheek,

about to wipe his kiss off
or rub it in, I cannot decide,
and think that beyond his smoke
I catch the unhappy smell of work,
in the way I might see a fish
flick through a brown stream
which on first looking in I thought
was water, and water only.

*

I take a leaf out of a book
  I listen to money singing

I find an attic to call my own
  I think about soldiers counting

I look through a ceiling-window
  I hear a rifle firing

I lie in an empty bed
  I dream of a heart beating

I turn my eyes inward
  I catch a woman flying

I see . . .

  *

I saw money in the distance
like an enormous wave,
its ragged lip
churning up bits of engine

bobbins, empty paint-pots,
chimneys, and toppling forward
with the packed roar of voices
together but incomprehensible,

though as they came closer
lessening, an ordinary shout
rushing into trenches,
oozing along gun-barrels

flash-flooding the bomb-sites
in city-centres, drowning rubble,
and all the time quieter,
gradually shrivelling

until not like a wave at all
but a strong and steady tide
dimpling across grazing,
swilling round new factories,

rising through wires and cables,
and filling computer screens
flashing their busy green numbers
in perfect silence. Perfect silence.

*

The roof over our heads
weighs so disastrously much
when it falls it will crush us all in our beds.

The world wants me to know
our children could reach up
and stave off this weight from us sheltering below.

Our children are asleep;
they have no idea
how fast this weight might drive us into the earth or how deep.

Our lives are our own.
Fall, roof, fall,
if that's what it takes to show me where I am most at home.

*

Last thing, I take out the empties.
There's frost on the doorstep,
frost on the paving-stones,
a skin of frost on the ash-buds
over-reaching the garden wall.

I'm tired, but just for now
I can feel the world is mine
for as little or much as I want;
I can lean against my house
and not even feel the cold.

Due south at the end of the street
the City of London's towers
are blinking their million eyes:
I can meet their level gaze
and pretend they are nothing to me.

My empties make their mark:
a brittle, nipped-off crash.
And still there's no one about.
Not a siren-song. Not a dog.
No breeze through the iron ash.

3 A Modern Ecstasy

When I was a boy with my father right behind me
he shooed me out one day in the early morning
with a gun tucked under my arm and said: Why not
walk round for an hour and see what you can find?

I followed our tatty hedge which led me past
the Ashground, then the pond filled in with bricks,
then the Council tip, and then the water-meadows
where I stopped, felt the emptiness, and wanted to go back.

I saw the hoar-frost sunlit on a line of sycamores
which staggered with the river in its twisting bed;
I heard the snow-crust hardening the grass which creaked
and grumbled as I flicked the safety-catch and moved ahead.

I hated it: the signs of people, then the lack of them;
the ugliness, and then that crystal beauty flooding in.
I don't know why. My feelings were my own.
My life was mine. My life was everything.

So when the hare appeared I didn't hesitate.
Before it cleared the line of sycamores I had it
covered, waiting for my moment, which was when
it sat down door-step still, the long ears brindled white,

the short-lashed eyes, the split and quizzical top lip all fixed
for ever as I bowled it over, so at any time thereafter
I might call them up, and see the blood-filled nose again,
the clotted fur, the gleaming brain wide open to the air

as I do now, tip-toeing forward through the bedroom dark
towards you in your cot to hear you breathe, to loom above
your milky-smelling body and your hare-lipped face
for no especial reason, just for love.

4   Lines of Desire

It starts with a father
who climbs his son
and weighs him down
begging to live:
it starts with love.

It starts with a roof
of paper money
the slightest breeze
might blow into space:
it starts with love.

It starts with a child
whose stitched-up face
is a whiskery cat
learning to smile:
it starts with love.

It starts with the word
you breathe in my ear
which enters my heart
with a thundering roar:
it starts with love.

*

This soldier I loved, the soldier seventy years younger than me:
when he died his widow wanted a silence where she might see
him again. She sent the children to her sister, drew the curtains,
lay in her bed, and ordered straw to be spread on the cobbles

outside, so that when wheels passed by, or horses, they would be no more than a whisper.

This lasted for years. Then the children came home, the curtains opened, the stamped-down straw blew away, and she had her life back, only it was never exactly her life again. She heard of a man who had known her soldier, and discovered him miles away in a locked room with one ceiling-window, nothing to read or listen to, and nothing he could break — nothing like a vase or a cup — because what could be broken might also be a weapon.

When she saw him a second time she took a map with her, to show off the country her soldier had known by heart. Now they sat on the bed in silence, ambling through springing woods, sliding down chalk banks, dabbling the brown water in gravel pits, and at the end of everything walking off side by side along a wide cart-track, each in their own dry runnel of mud, a low grass wall between them but nevertheless like lovers, letting the track take them wherever it wanted, leaving no footprints.

*

They are my mother and father,
this couple walking before me,
each in the rut of a cart-track
somewhere deep in the country.

My father is home on leave
with pollen-dust on his toe-caps;
my mother's legs are bare
and flecked with bright straw-scratches.

It's years before I am born
and they've still to imagine me;
I'm merely the ghost in the hedge-row
which might be the wind or a bird.

I'm bound to stay behind them
all day while the cart-track dawdles
here and there past chalk-pits
and sullen, green-eyed ponds.

I only leave when I've seen her
working her hand through his arm,
when I've heard him speak her name
in a whisper like never before.

*

Right at the back
half-listening
half-dreaming
I open my eyes
in the dusty classroom
to learn about love
and Marcus Brutus
an honourable man
clanks off the page
his judicious tongue
swelling out of his mouth
to roll the earth
in a new direction
and raise a wave
on its buried lakes.

Then I shut my eyes
on the swirling dark
of lunatic atoms
and Portia appears
in a moonlit garden
of holly and ice
which is bitter to see
but never so painful
as she is herself
who has swallowed fire
which fills her mouth
and her long throat
then drops clean through
to her sizzling heart
and won't go out.

Then I open my eyes
on Brutus once more
and discover by now
he has learnt about love
and thrown himself down
on his stupid sword
while the air rocks
in my dusty classroom
and silence falls
so deep I can hear
the earth return
on its creaking axle
to just where it was
and a wave die down
on its buried lakes.

*

Dum dum de dum, de dum de dum de start
clack clackety clack, clack clackety clack clack see
diddle di da da, diddle di da da heart.

Clack clackety clack, clack clackety clack clack burn
diddle di da da, diddle di da da me
dum dum de dum, de dum de dum de learn.

Diddle di da da, diddle di da da give
dum dum de dum, de dum de dum de free
clack clackety clack, clack clackety clack clack live.

*

Then I met you and was lifted up from the world
once more, up from our bed, up through the roof
and into the air, the air which touched us lightly
as cloth, yet also seemed solid and heavy as water.

We circled a while, inspecting the streets we knew –
the pavements crazed with familiar cracks, the square
which is really a circle, the plane trees
raising their dusty hands to snatch at our feet –

but we were free, and spreading our wings
swooped off to a different part of the city
where sirens wept, and crowds of querulous faces
loomed like coins in a fountain, except they were shouting,

until we flew on, and reached that zig-zag line
which marks the edge of the town, the scrap yards
and unfinished houses where street lamps take long strides
then end, and the moon comes out at last

soaking the huddles of woodland, the hedges
sprinting for cover, the white-washed gabled farms –
and stopped, both of us treading the air
and staring silently down at the country below,

finding the easily overlooked tracks,
the secret runnels, the pathways buried in grass,
the short cuts and fenced-off lanes, the lines of desire,
the furtive steps up hillsides or deep under trees –

as if every footprint that we had set down on the world
were still to be seen, and we could be sure
which trails we had followed were false, which true,
and where we were lost before we came into our own.

   *

starling-song

from the telephone wire
plugged into my house

down

scratchy-dry this late dusk
but sweet still while I wait

here

on my worn doorstep to catch you
last thing over the threshold

now

body and fixed listening head
like a tuning fork tingling

soon

the note bubbling
then steady in my own throat

  *

Home –
shaking office-smoke from your hair,
the unhappy money-taste on your skin:
wherever you are, I will be there too.

Kitchen –
eyes closing and mouth sunk into a pout,
tongue stumbling between food and talk:
wherever you are, I will be there too.

Bedroom –
winded silk shirt collapsing on to a chair,
tights too spindly and thin to make it:
wherever you are, I will be there too.

Bedside –
picking across the miles of difficult carpet,
air-current holding you up but only just:
wherever you are, I will be there too.

Bed –
beautiful heavy marionette with your strings cut,
then tightening as you roll over to face me:
wherever you are, I will be there too.

*

In their universe above my head
our children are gunning each other down,
hunting the enemy from doorway to doorway,
braining a doll on the stairs, up-ending a box
of rocket launchers and tanks: *clank clankety clank.*

I am at work in my room underground,
my pen itching a sheet of paper,
dreaming up ways to stop the roof falling,
then pushing my chair back and staring
at nothing on earth: *dum dum de dum.*

Into my head flows a crooked stream
with sycamores flourishing round it,
a flat meadow of frozen grass,
and a hare which staggers when my shot hits
but darts off perfect and unbloodied: *hey nonny.*

*

I came to the edge of the world –
where the crumbling sky
rests on the roof-tops all day drizzling lead,
where the acid sea
has bleached the pink from gulls' feet,
where the exhausted smoking earth
grows nothing.

It happened today.

I wanted to give you my love but when I tried I couldn't get
                                                        through,
so I left my hotel and walked along the coast road into the city:
the rain fell hard, stinging my face,
and steamed-up taxis slowed as they drew level then sped off
                                                        honking.

I found an empty bar and another telephone
but the lines were still down, and when I craned into the
                                                        darkness
I could hear the miles crackle, could see the wind and sleet
                                        filling the spaces between us.

You were nowhere,
and when I shut my eyes tight
I felt rooted into that sour ground.
I could even sense the earth
turning,
the fire at its heart nearly out,
the cold
seeping through galleries of black stone
into the soles of my shoes.

I gave up
and walked back into the rain.
You were somewhere,
I knew that, at least, not here but somewhere,
and I would find you
as long as I went on looking.

I came to the market square in the old town
and my feet rang on the huge glistening cobbles
while beneath me soldiers still fought hand to hand
along sewers and stinking barrel-vaulted drains.

Above my head the chipped bell in the bell-tower
still sent its flat message into the countryside
and a man crossing his farmyard suddenly hesitated,
looked up, then hurried indoors for his rifle.

In front of me the pastel-coloured houses rose:
a ragged wave, still swirling the lives of their fathers,
mothers and children, their sheets, hearthstones, carpets,
everything down on me to sweep me away.

When I found a path through
I was on the old road again,
the one winding back to my hotel
along the dockyard wall,
bringing me out at last on the beach
so I knew where I was.

My shoes sank into the sand, and the rain redoubled its efforts,
yet when I reached the pier and saw the lights of my hotel
shining ahead of me weakly but plainly,
I nevertheless turned aside and walked out over the water,
to the slipped-tile hut where the wind was fiercer than ever,
the waves a darker brown and more turbulent, the cloud
                                        thicker,
and the few gargoyle-fishermen too sad to pay me any
                                        attention.

I did this purposefully,
as though I had a reason.

As though the fishermen might speak to me
in a language I could admire.

As though they might tell me it was true
the soldiers had laid down their weapons.

As though everything I knew to be complicated
was in fact easy.

As though the price of everything
had finally been agreed.

As though the past was really the past
and I had escaped it.

As though I could grip the rail with both hands,
lean over,
and see the waves change from brown to translucent blue,
the wind drop,
and you,
at liberty in the clear water of your own life,
with oxygen slithering from your mouth and nose
and water-ropes twisting from your fingers and toes,
rising steadily towards me through the reflection of my face.

JOE SOAP

One

A soldier might be talking cheese
with the man in the moon,
and still feel at home by naming names:
Nineveh, Upton, Brailes, Winter Ridge,
Knollands, Idlicote, Scorpion, Fell Mill.

He might hurtle over a waterfall
crouched in a splitting barrel,
and still be a child learning to swim:
Stour, Wagtail, Tus, Staucchill Ditch,
Chalybeate, Sur, Cod, Black Brook.

He might stall a truck in the desert
with nothing between his head and the sun,
and still feel the dewfall in a bluebell wood:
Blackthorn, Wittycombe, Shear, Hell Brake,
Battleton, Spencer's, Fox, Graveground Coppice.

He might launch off into sheer space
from the pinnacle of an ice-mountain,
and still descend to safety slope by slope:
Bush, Shenlow, Rough, Sun Rising,
Long, Orchard, Edgehill, Crimscote Down.

He might take the wrong way through fog
any time in his life without warning,
and still know which road he wanted:
Epwell, Preston, Armscote, Fosse Way,
Christmas, Preston, Sugarswell, Jacob's Ladder.

*

Our reference: B2715

Warwickshire Constabulary
Shipston-upon-Stour Police Station
Stratford Road

Date: 4 January 1918

Statement taken by: PC 407 Smith
From: Joseph Soap (Captain)

I first met Captain T. A. (Thomas) Atkins four months ago, in September of the year 1917 (one thousand nine hundred and seventeen) when he joined the Manchester Regiment for training in Ripon, West Riding of Yorkshire. I was temporarily stationed there. I had first joined the regiment in the year 1916 (one thousand nine hundred and sixteen). I have served mainly in France since then. At Christmas 1917 (one thousand nine hundred and seventeen) we were given one week's leave, beginning on 24 December. Captain Atkins invited me to say with him at St Stephen's Farm, his father's home. He knew that I had no home of my own to go to. St Stephen's Farm is situated approximately 5 (five) miles north-east of Shipston-upon-Stour, Warwickshire. We arrived there on the evening of the same day that our leave began.

At 9.30 a.m. on 3 January 1918 (one thousand nine hundred and eighteen) Captain Atkins and I informed his father Michael Atkins and sister Margaret Atkins that we intended to go ferreting for rabbits. We left the house shortly afterwards. I carried a 12 (twelve) bore shot gun belonging to Michael Atkins, and a bag of cartridges. Michael Atkins accompanied us to the stables on the northern side of the farm yard. He took 2 (two) ferrets from their cage in one of the stables. He put the ferrets into a sack, which he then passed to Captain Atkins. Captain Atkins and I left Michael Atkins in the stables. It was a fine day. Captain Atkins was in good spirits. We walked along a cart-track in a south-westerly direction for approximately 20 (twenty) minutes. We reached Staunchill Ditch, the boundary between St Stephen's Farm and Upton Farm. The Ditch is a narrow stream running from west to east along the southern edge of a field of grazing. Across the stream from the field, the ground rises into an embankment, 10 (ten) feet high. This embankment is thickly covered with brambles.

I handed Captain Atkins the cartridges and gun, which at this stage was still unloaded. Captain Atkins then passed me the sack containing the ferrets. I climbed over the Ditch. I put on a pair of thick gloves. I dragged the brambles away from several rabbit holes. I took the ferrets from the sack and put them into separate holes. When I had finished doing this it was approximately 10 a.m.

The ferrets disappeared underground, and shortly afterwards I heard squealing from inside the embankment. A rabbit emerged from one of the entrances I had cleared. It jumped the Ditch and ran into the field towards Captain Atkins. Captain Atkins shot and killed the rabbit.

We proceeded in this fashion for approximately 15 (fifteen) minutes. Captain Atkins shot several more rabbits during this time, and became increasingly excited. He shouted out to me on a number of occasions, and once or twice ran up and down in the field. I do not remember exactly what he said, and I do not believe that he kept the safety catch of his gun 'on' while he was running. The grass in the field was long. It had been raining the previous night, and was slippery.

When I could no longer hear the ferrets underground, I

prepared to take them out of the holes. I knelt down and turned my back to Captain Atkins in order to do this. As I was tying the ferrets into the sack, I heard a shot behind me. I called out to Captain Atkins, telling him to stop shooting. There was no answer. I looked over my shoulder and saw Captain Atkins lying in the grass. He was face down. He was not moving. I immediately went to his side. His arms were stretched out beneath him, holding the gun. I spoke his name. He did not reply. I looked underneath him. His right hand was clasped round the trigger-guard of the gun. His left hand was round the barrel. The shot had entered his head beneath the chin. He was not breathing. I knew that he was dead. The time was approximately 10.30 a.m.

I made no attempt to move Captain Atkins. I ran back at once to St Stephen's Farm. I found Michael Atkins outside his house, in the yard. I told him what had happened. Mr Atkins became very distressed. He told his daughter to notify the police. He then collected a hand-cart from the stables and returned with me to the field where Captain Atkins lay. We put the body of Captain Atkins on the hand-cart. We also put the gun and the sack containing the ferrets on the cart. We then wheeled the cart to St Stephen's Farm. We reached the farm at 11.30 a.m. and found the police waiting.

Signed

Captain Joseph Soap

*

Tommy and I went walking
Out that Christmas leave –
Tommy no more than a raw recruit
And me a soldier brave –

A-walking down a cart track
Of ribbed and rained-on clay,
To waste whatever time we had
Before we vanished away.

Tommy stood up behind me,
Adventure on his mind;
I put my hand inside the earth
To see what I could find.

Nothing; nothing; nothing:
Black light and mud-cold air –
Though buried somewhere out of sight
Death lay in wait, and terror.

Now I won't tell you any more –
Just my rank and number.
Tommy died in an accident.
What else should I remember?

*

From the *Birmingham Post*, 3 February 1918

TRAGIC ACCIDENT
by a Staff Reporter

A verdict of accidental death has been returned in the case of
Captain T. A. (Thomas) Atkins, 18, the son of Mr Michael
Atkins of St Stephen's Farm, Shipston-upon-Stour, whom we
reported as having died of gun-shot wounds on 3 January this
year. Giving evidence, Captain J. Soap of the Manchester
Regiment, a friend of the deceased, said that Captain Atkins
had slipped and fallen while out shooting rabbits. There were
no suspicious circumstances.

Captain Atkins had himself recently joined the Manchesters, and was soon to be posted overseas, where all who knew him expected him to prove a gallant officer. As well as his father, he leaves a younger sister, Margaret (15).

*

Joe Soap took the train back to camp at Ripon. Everyone there knew about the shooting and the inquest, but no one mentioned it to him. This was not surprising. No one looked to Captain Soap for talk, even though people were suspicious. Perhaps Atkins had killed himself – that would have been cowardice; perhaps the Captain was covering up for his friend? Joe said nothing. Nothing about Atkins, nothing about anything else. He had no family to speak of, no place to come from or return to, no stories of his life before the war.

Earlier, in France, certain things had come to light. Joe Soap had been brave. He had been dutiful. And he had been silent. His fellows began by resenting him, then got used to him; he had no friends, and no enemies either. If he had been killed, no one would have missed him.

But he was not killed. For almost two years, at the end of an attack, or after a night of shelling, there would be other faces missing, and other names to cross off lists; never his. In peace time, people might have called him heartless. In France it never came to that. He was a person who was not a person. He could have been anyone.

Days turned into weeks, and weeks into months. Then in early summer the German army in France made a rapid advance west. At home, new recruits were mobilized, and troops in training were put on alert. Captain Soap travelled south with other men from his battalion. He crossed the English Channel at night, expecting to meet the enemy as soon as he landed, but discovered that everything had changed. The

German advance had faltered; German troops were retreating. The Manchesters were ordered south-east to join the 4th Army. After three days' marching, they reached Vendelles.

Captain Soap had a batman, Private Doe. On the outskirts of Vendelles, Doe found a large, intact garden shed, suspended an oil lamp from the central beam, and arranged a writing table. The captain sat at the table censoring letters for two hours, then lay on his straw bed watching the stars through a hole in the roof. There was no mist, and only moderate shelling in the distance.

The smell of the hay was ticklish, but it made him drowsy. The night before, billeted in a ruined house 25 miles north, he had listened to men nearby singing 'The Muffin Man of Armentières', until a shell had dropped unexpectedly close, making the plaster rattle down inside the wall behind his head, and blowing out his lamp. Then he had heard shouts, and a chaotic scrabbling. Now there was no panic, nothing urgent. The stars through the roof grew closer together, swarming into a thin, overall veil.

By 4.30 next morning he was marching again, due east, the men packed around him in a block which stretched whenever a staff car went past, or a motorbike. As the sun came up, the clouds started to drizzle, so there was no gold or red to look at, nothing to cheer him. Another barrage began in the distance. The rain increased.

Then the road flattened and the battalion entered a new country. There was sloppy mud under Joe's boots – and stacked on either side of him, sometimes in neat piles, sometimes in collapsing mounds, the bodies of dead soldiers. Most were several days old, the skin of their faces hollow and famished. At the bottom of the heaps, faces were a darker colour and beginning to decompose. Maggots lived in some of the eyes and mouths. Jaws had been broken by the weight heaped above, and long bones had slewed loose, surprisingly white. Whatever the stages of their decay, all these soldiers looked the same. Enemy. Friend. Enemy. Friend. At the top of each stack, however, the bodies looked more familiar. Joe saw a crinkly-haired man in a tight British uniform, his hands clasping his belly as if he was supporting a chuckle. And a ratty-faced man wearing a pair of schoolmaster's wire-framed spectacles: one of the lenses had shivered.

Rising from them all, hanging in a low cloud and yellowing the air, was a sickly-sweet stench. Some of the marching soldiers waved their hands in front of their faces: 'Waaauuufff'. Others tilted their heads back and took short, fastidious breaths. Joe stared at his boots, flecked with grey mud turning to white as it dried, and watched them moving. Left, right. Left, right.

The battalion reached Swiss Cottage in the late afternoon, advancing quickly across ground they had won inch by inch the previous year, and came to a line of abandoned German trenches. The barrage continued on the horizon.

The men were dismissed and flocked into the trenches, crowding their corridors and runnels, roosting in low rooms from which everything valuable had been removed. Private Doe led Captain Soap down a wooden ladder into a space where cooking fires were sizzling. Someone was singing. It was like a holiday. The barrage kept up its thunder and earth-shovelling. The enemy would be moving troops up to face them in the morning.

Joe ducked into his billet, where an oil lamp was already burning. He saw a row of pine roof-props – the bark had been stripped off each one, and the pale wood was grimy where hands had gripped it. To the left: a table. To the right: two sets of bunks, professionally made. Three more officers crowded in behind, and Joe greeted them with a nod, then lay down on one of the lower bunks. He locked his hands behind his head. In a moment he would eat, then there would be more letters to censor.

Two hours later, Joe stretched out again. Cigarette smoke drooped from the bunk above him, and he faced away from the room towards the dark mud wall. There was a square hole cut into the earth in front of him, a miniature door. Joe put his right hand into the hole, his skin prickling – but there was nothing. Cold air. Colder mud. His fingers worked round the entire space. It was empty. No. Not empty. A leathery hardness. Paper. A book.

He drew it out, holding the spine towards the light. It was a bible, and when Joe opened it he read inside:

T.

24 February 1917,
his birthday
with love.

He softly snapped the book shut. Someone, a German soldier, must have taken this off someone, an English soldier, and stowed it here as booty. Joe looked at his fingers: his nails were bitten. Then he opened the bible once more – this time in the middle, at random. He read: '1. A false balance is abomination to the Lord: but a just weight is his delight. 2. When pride cometh, then cometh shame: but with the lowly is wisdom.' He could not understand what it meant. He flipped the bible back into its hole for someone else to find, and fell asleep. The barrage stopped.

There were no changes in the sky to show when dawn became day. One minute Joe was dreaming, the next he was awake and dipping outside into the trench. The dark air tasted of copper. There had been a frost, and fragments of ice glittered in the mud. He could sense men fidgeting in the darkness around him, pressing down their helmets, running hands over their rifles. His memory stirred, and he almost remembered something – something that had happened when he was a child – then lay still. His only life was his life now. He was no one except this person he had become.

The barrage began again at 6.00 a.m., shells whining from the guns behind them, shrieking as they arched overhead, then falling in a jagged line among the enemy trenches ahead. It lasted for an hour. At 7.00 a.m. a whistle blew – a school noise, Joe realized, fighting it but helpless to resist. The soldiers on either side of him clattered up the trench wall as if lessons were over and they had been turned loose. After their obedient silence they were allowed to do anything. They could scream as much as they liked, and fall down in the mud, and race about shouting. Joe climbed up a vertical ladder and also began running. In the corners of his eyes he could see some men keeping step with him, and others still screaming and tumbling into the mud. None of them made any impression on him. He was invisible now, and weightless – pressing easily forward even though the air didn't want this. It raged at him, desperate to block his way.

Joe Soap vanished. As he lifted his head to the horizon to see whether the sun had grown larger, whether it had climbed free of its grey mud-sill, a shell leapt down precisely in front of him. That was when he vanished. One minute he was running, sweating, glancing up; the next he was nothing. Another minute more, and some of the other soldiers – his friends who were not his friends – were stumbling into the trenches he had been running towards. Then the guns stopped firing and the barrage lifted. Time passed. Men were sent back to collect the wounded, and to pile up the dead. Nothing remained of Joe Soap. He had been on the earth, and then he was not on the

earth. He had been a person, then he was no longer a person.
He might not have existed.

*

I had already come to the utmost edge of myself
when I was hurtled out into nowhere at all.

    I am here in the world
    broken apart
    alone and apart,
    never again as myself.

I had already reached the extreme end of the earth
when it swerved away and left me milling in space.

    I can fall to the ground
    one piece at a time
    any moment in time,
    never again as myself.

I had already divided up my brain into pieces
when my whole body shattered and went up in smoke.

    I can come back and live
    whenever I like
    as whatever I like,
    never again as myself.

I had already snapped all my connections with life
when life ended and what happened next began.

I can speak in my voice
in a hundred tongues
without moving my tongue,
never again as myself.

Two

I first fell to earth
a whole sea and half a continent away from the country
                                    of my birth:

not even myself, Joe,
but Johanna – just so;

in Germany,
winter 1933;

a timber-merchant's wife
at the start of my life

but God! buried in thick woods, fifty miles out from Berlin,
and pregnant – which means lying asleep all day or just
                                    lying in,

which means nothing.
No, which means waiting. That's something.

*

He is off with his cronies today, my husband,
but the house he built crouches over me just the same,
its steeply pitched roof turning the sky solid
now that wind suddenly roars at me after a silence.

Supposing I let this wind catch and lift me –
or somehow climbed it; suppose I was floating
above myself, and could look down and see
just where I am, how I got here, what here means.

There'd be an ocean of trees, that's all:
pine-tips like wave-points lashed white,
the track to town bedded under a needle-blanket,
and in all the world no sign of another light.

Of course I exaggerate, of course. *Haaaaaahhh*.
When I breathe on the window above the kitchen sink,
intricate frost-flowers soften slowly and show
the yard outside curly with shavings, and further

his moss-tiled, falling-to-bits wooden shed.
Through its open door
the blind eye of a pine rocking-horse
bobs out then back as the wind grabs and lets go.

*

A gang of his shirts
swells on the line
as the wind still
streams from the pines.

Look at it now,
a rattling rush:
wet sleeves roll up,
pigeon chests puff.

Crack!
without heads
they take on the world,
they wish it dead.

Crack!
stinging air
has hurled the sun
any old where.

On the skyline behind them
clouds race for cover.
No sheltering now.
Cold light all over.

*

Now he is home, puffed up with life in the world.
How it is better. How he is stronger.
How money sweats. How they will build
a dead straight road through the woods to the north of here.

While I listen, wind peels off from an axe
swishing close to my face. Hot.
But it's cold – colder now there's no storm
and frost over everything, holding the whole world still.

It has smacked each blade of grass on the head,
jammed the bolt in the yard-gate,
fallen head over heels in the horse trough,
lost its temper, and left the water in chaos.

I don't understand. Who are these people
he tells me have lost their homes
and now have to live in the wilderness?
Why is he out in the gloom

when he should be with me in the warm?
Tomorrow would do – but there he goes
crack, crack, fixing a soldier's head on a stick,
then planing the curve of the rocking-horse neck.

In the air still hardening over us both
sunlight is starting to rot between leaves.
The sun in its place. Leaves in their place.
Half the earth always dark as it twirls in space.

*

My weighted step
halts at the threshold:
something is sick
out in the world.

Voices arrive
on the sinking breeze;
pine needle tongues
hoarse with news.

How a charging hoard
more room! more room!
flooded the ghetto
more room! more room!

How a factory gate
squealed and locked:
You! You are chosen.
You! You are not.

How a line of waggons
snivelled and stank
the day it paused
at our local halt.

How what I do
is watch light fall
from the doorway here.
Nothing else at all.

＊

A voice isn't a whole person – ridiculous, it can't be –
but this one wants to rule my life, and jack-knifes
at night-fall out of the wireless to stick upright
here at my feet in front of the stove, still arguing.

Blood, it wants, *blood* – and *Room, more room! Room!*
ripping through towns I know but have never seen,
slicing off chimneys, shattering windows,
blasting locks apart, deafening men, women and children

who run fast but not fast enough and cannot escape,
slicing veins in wrists, splitting heads wide open,
never relenting, even swaying the tops of trees here,
here which is nowhere, where the voice becomes patient

but still wants something, wants me to say *Yes! Yes!*
when it will stop. Stop dead. Stand still quivering.
Then step forward with an armful of white alpine flowers
and a kiss for my unborn but obviously beautiful child.

＊

Hosannah! I did no more than open my eyes
and it thawed: not outside – not in the night like this,
the bedroom window still thickening with frost –
but in me: a gush, a sudden spring welling.

Hilarious! But I was cold, and sent him out
into the yard for firewood, his life for a moment
all mine and my life no longer my own,
impatient at what seemed like hours, a desertion.

Though in fact nothing like it. Fumbling back,
arms awkward round shock-ended logs,
then trying to set them down by the hearth quietly
and failing, making this mad slapstick clatter,

he said when he'd picked up the first half dozen
a snake had flicked at him out of the wood-pile,
sizzling, an adder he thought, but so small, so quick,
who knows, and he wasn't sure whether the log he threw

hurt it or not, or where it had wriggled away to now,
only that he would have liked to bring it to me and show
the dead expressionless head, the copper eye, the tongue,
the skid-marked skin like the place where something went
wrong.

＊

Then the small hours, my own body loathing me,
walls sweating, the greasy ceiling slithering
under my feet, eyes backwards, a metal bowl
turning inside out until I am empty.

Then a pause. A delay. Then one careful breath
then another, fitting the walls and ceiling together.
Then back to full stretch on the wrecked sheet
once more, and yelling my head off, and him

rushing in from the yard. Then the gymnast voice
leaping out of the wireless again and sticking
not in the floorboards this time, eager, but inside me.
What opens up is another long view of the world

fizzing through space, a view I have seen before,
only never like this: washed-out skies,
continents bare, complex seas sprawling,
rebuilding, then wind-whipped and charging

forwards, but barren now – no fish, no sails
breaking their white expressionless distances, nothing,
a nothing the voice created, in love with itself,
but slavers through still, scouring for signs of life.

*

Next thing I sleepwalk
wide awake,
free falling
clean through daybreak,

the roof-beam down
on my juddering heart,
the trees pouring in
but I never hurt,

and my poor head
– what's inside my head –
torn out of me,
out, out of my bed

– she's mine! – and off,
away in the world,
her gimcrack body
slippy with blood,

racing too fast
for me to catch up
now I'm less than myself,
and fuddled with love.

*

A cloud crawls over the early sun
and look: it brings her every possible grief.
She's aghast; she's an eel half out of her skin.
Light comes back, she unfolds, and is blissfully still.

This makes me think: she could know all she needed to know
without moving from here. Columns of marching soldiers –
those will be lines engraved on her face;
trainloads of suffering eyes – those are her tears

which fill up her ears in her rage. Her tears; her ears –
so stupid. You hear? I can no longer say what I mean
and make it sound true. Her ears. You hear?
There is no longer room for it all. *Crack. Crack.*

When I straighten my back, my head slams out
through the roof. It's a beautiful day.
Pine needles jab at the sun.
A shining wind jumps up, sliding over our house and on.

*

This is only the start
and now, today,
I wring out the world,
it wrings out me.

Squeeze; squeeze:
a thread of silk
spins from my heart,
more blood than milk.

This is only the start
and now her scream
strikes like the sound
of my own name.

Squeeze; squeeze:
her widening eye
has emptied my brain
of all it knew.

This is only the start
and now I would choose
to die for her life.
Squeeze; squeeze.

Three

The second time I fell to earth
was thousands of miles east and a few thousand more further
                                                    south:

and this time myself, Joe,
plain Joe;

place: Masjhid-i-Suliman,
Iran;

date: spring 1954;
purpose: I knew precisely what I had come for –

to build a pipeline carrying oil,
and of course to get my young life under sail.

(Absurd to say 'sail' when I'm talking about desert;
I mean getting life started. Getting the life I want.)

*

Here is history, lest we forget. There was a war and life below
decks with plenty of cigarettes and no sun. When I climbed out
into the peaceful light at last, I was an engineer on course for
dry land. I went home first, with nothing better to do, then to
America. Eventually I reached Elk City, Oklahoma, two
hundred miles from the nearest table-cloth, then I came here.
    Here I have survived revolution and sunburn, and I know
which I'd rather have. I have fallen asleep with boredom at a
dinner table, and on another day dropped down exhausted

with work. I have filled my shoes with sand below sea level, and strained my back in the zig-zag mountains. I have spent days in silence, and helped to invent a new language. All this means I could tell you about wells and wild cats. Roughnecks and roustabouts. Spudding in. A gusher, if you're unlucky. Fishing, if you're unlucky again. A round trip – and mud, which half kills you. Then we could talk about pay, and not knowing whether it's close or a lifetime away. Yes, I will tell you all that, which is history too, lest we forget.

*

I have to admit when I first arrived I hardly saw anything in it. The desert and the mountains, the sun, the fires at night: I looked them over like someone examining a false mirror, trying to squint past my own face and glimpse another face watching me. For instance – outside the back door I found the Phoenicians, sweating under bales of wool. They were deciding it was hopeless, and turning back. Another time I saw Alexander, his breast-plate blazing in the midday heat. No, this didn't happen all the time.

And once I took a nap on the verandah and I heard the well-heads drinking. Steady, slow-tongued gulps. The sound a man would make if he had managed to escape the desert and collapse in one more mirage, which he found was true. I heard this, then I saw the hills around me suddenly split open. Thousands of white faces crowded through – faces, arms and legs; hands and fingers; teeth; eyeballs. All swept past me headlong on this river out of nowhere. Not a water-river, naturally. I don't have to tell you that. As I said, I only see what's there.

*

At first I might have said 'home'. Now I would say house.

Four-walls-and-a-roof. Whatever. Place in the middle of no-where. As if the idea of home had dropped from an aeroplane into the heart of the desert, not caring what happened next. What happened next was a second house, then a third, then enough for a street, then a halt. The dead straight road leading north through the mountains, south to the coast. That's all.

This is history, lest we forget. I mean: this is me in the days when I knew almost nothing and thought I had nothing to learn. My orders? Build a pipeline to run from the mountains 300 miles to the sea. Then find an island somewhere. Why? So they could build a refinery. So there'd be ships. So there'd be money – money to make the world go round.

And round the world went – although at the end of my very first day, I thought I had lost my balance. I found a makeshift removals van, blocking the path to my door. The walnut veneer on my desk as they heaved it inside! A jangling bedframe scratching the new-made floor! When the van disappeared I sat for what might have been hours, with wind sliding in through holes in the wall. The wind like a hand which runs over everything – *now this is mine; will you fight me, or what* – and the sun on its perch one moment then suddenly gone. Which is when you begin to see fires.

*

There used to be the pure wilderness of rock and sky;
now there is a game of scaffolding, and roads unravelling:
wherever next in the world,
and when?

There used to be wind rushing hither and yon as it chose;
now there are false starts, and gusts swerving down alleys:
wherever next in the world,
and when?

There used to be dazzle trapped in the eye of an oil puddle;
now there are lights all night, and silver refinery towns:
                    wherever next in the world,
                              and when?

There used to be silence stretching all the way up to the sun;
now there are pumps squeaking, and builders yelling orders:
                    wherever next in the world,
                              and when?

There used to be high valleys even the birds said no to;
now there are signposts, and a price for every grain of sand:
                    wherever next in the world,
                              and when?

There used to be me alone, lighting a match in the dark;
now there are flames, and a view into infinite space:
                    wherever next in the world,
                              and when?

                    *

You didn't know I was married. You know now. For years she
went home, when our girl was a baby, and that was all right.
There were letters. Things out here just are as they are. I had
my pipeline to build; my island to find. It wasn't for ever. And
now she is back.
    About those fires. There's oil so close to the surface you'd
think the desert was floating and everyone on it was floating
too: adrift, precarious, having to sink or swim — except of
course it is catching alight that worries you, nothing to do with
water. One cigarette. One flash of heat from a window. A bird.
A beetle rubbing its hands. Sometimes it seems just thinking
about them starts them off. You close your eyes. The darkness

thickens. You wait. Then – mind! – a fountain of flames shoots out of a boulder, a cactus, a pebble.

You see what I mean about sunset. As soon as it's done, I can stand at my window and there in the darkness are dozens of fires. Some tall – ridiculous, rangy fellows who fool and flap their arms; most small. Candles which grow in the earth, or so I once thought. Now I'm not sure. They're more like sobs and sighs – half rage, half sorrow, which used to be secret but now are the light of our lives.

*

Well, I got my work under way, then came the revolution. What was the revolution? The revolution was the earth turning. It was winter, not spring. Frost, not warmth. Dark, not sunlight. It was a voice insisting *here* not *here*. It was *more room!* It was Mossadeq, wiping his hand across his chin, loosening his tie, then buckling down with his whole weight against the Peacock Throne. He had a crowd behind him, lending the whole of their weight also, so eventually the throne budged, *here* became *here*, sunlight pierced my head from a different angle, blinding me, and for a while I was driven out.

When I came back, the earth had spun round again. No Mossadeq, another war over, and my life set clear before me. Which brings me at once to the nomads. The first thing I knew they were grazing my doorstep, calling it theirs. How could I have known? Should I have asked the thistles who was their master? Should I have questioned a stone? Each spring after that, I would watch for them clattering in from the mountains, then drive to the boundary-river to see them cross: a rag-tag tribe, on makeshift oil-drum rafts. To see. To welcome them back. They knew they had only to lean one hand on the world to make it move. I had only to knock on the solid rock to shatter it, then see it flow.

Just because I hardly mention her, it doesn't mean she isn't
here. She's always here, except when she's away. You follow
me? Just take today. At noon I came home from the office (call
it office, call it home) for nothing but to see her and because it's
spring, which sweeps across us here like rain, a sudden
downpour, one day nothing and the next a green degree to
everything, so no one knows quite whether to be sad or happy,
or how long they've got to be whatever they decide.

I'd chosen happiness. I liked the dust-film on my wind-
screen, driving back. I liked the way my shoes made soft
explosions in the sand around our gate. I even liked the midge-
troupe fizzing underneath the pines. I stopped, and watched
the garden sprinkler bend its peacock feathers forwards,
backwards, forwards, always threatening to touch first me and
then the house then me but never reaching.

You were close, you had to be. You'd left your stripey towel
in the sun, still crumpled with the shape of you. Your
ribbonless straw hat was there. Your book flat on its back, a
tuft of pages standing up. I knew I only had to call and you'd
appear, but I did nothing. I just stood there – sunlight
drumming on my back, the water-feathers hissing, midges
rising, falling, rising. Then I crept away as I had come,
unlocked the office and went back to work.

*

There used to be the pure wilderness of rock and sky;
now there is a game of scaffolding, and roads unravelling:
          wherever next in the world,
                    and when?

There used to be jackal music under the freezing stars;
now there are porch lights, and bottles clinking on steps:
        wherever next in the world,
            and when?

There used to be a spring river's just-audible rush;
now there are swimming-pool shouts, and doors' slick locks:
        wherever next in the world,
            and when?

There used to be straight lines in sand and perfect circles;
now there are blocked exits, turnings back, veerings:
        wherever next in the world,
            and when?

There used to be a bare white island diving into sheer blue;
now there are tankers sidling, and reefs of smashed shell:
        wherever next in the world,
            and when?

There used to be me alone under the clear sky up to heaven;
now there are vapour trails and sea-urchin satellites staring:
        wherever next in the world,
            and when?

*

I found my island: Kharg Island, Kharg meaning it was made
of cowrie shells. I set my heart on it. We all did in the business,
seeing how it lay there in the gulf. A jewel. We could run our
pipelines out. Build our town-refinery. Call up tankers. No,
not like a jewel. More like a needle's eye to squeeze through if I
wanted to approach the kingdom.

    I first set foot there with the family, and of course it wasn't like a needle or a jewel. It was like a whale. A monstrous bow-back stopped in mid-descent but likely to begin its headlong downward charge again at any second. Yes, we all thought that – my wife, our little girl, myself – which meant we had to hurry – quick! quick! – before it pulled us underwater and we drowned.

Besides, there was the sun, the sun which turned the thin skin of the island into crackling. Half an hour, and we no longer saw the things in front of us, but others, somewhere else. My daughter, now, she found a tank had churned towards her through the sand, its gun and turret slick with oil. I said: impossible. All right, she said, head nodding, half asleep, and then: What's that? I told her: nothing – though in fact I'd rolled a shell between my fingers and drawn blood.

*

Just when everything seemed perfect. Just when the pipeline was finished. Just when pay seemed around the corner . . .

I'm talking about Red and Boots – and listen, there's no mystery to this. We had a monstrous fire: hundred foot flames, a giant octopus bagging the whole sky, and a derrick melted and sunk down its well like a wick in a candle. I knew at a glance it was miles beyond us. It had to be Red and Boots.

They flew in from Texas and set to with hardly a how-do-you-do. There was no time to lose, you see. I saw. They hired a bulldozer, welded a shield to the cab, stuck on a pair of enormous wobbling arms and gave them a stick of explosive to hold. Then Red climbed in and drove at the heart of the blaze. With this going on, Boots squirted him hard with a hose, straight-faced in his metal hat, like a child allowed to do something which breaks the rules.

What happened next was the dynamite stick exploding right over the well-head, a vacuum forming, and the fire going out. I mean, that's what happened at last, with most of our dynamite gone, Boots minus his eyebrows, Red half-fried in his cab, and the earth transformed from somewhere that's ours into somewhere no life belongs. All the same, it was nothing I couldn't explain. What did seem strange was how, when I finally brought Red home for a meal, I discovered my wife dolled up in the doorway to greet us, wearing a ten gallon hat.

*

A mouse might be famous for a day, and so might I. The mouse might roll a grain of wheat into his nest, and feel that now the worst can happen and he's lived his life. I might dream a pipeline springing from the wells on mountain-tops – a pipe which swoops to meet the desert, races in a single flat-eared streak towards the sea, then disappears, then rises on Kharg Island where the shells have long since vanished and the tankers fidget in impatient queues.

I dreamed it, measured it, then made it. Ninety thousand yards of pipe. Three thousand ton-weight links. One thousand men. Machinery to make the earth cave in. And at the coast a sort of armadillo upside-down, which as its paws were struggling in mid-air would push the pipeline forward, sliding it into the sea, more like something being born than something drowning.

There's a film of me in shallow water at the island end, all bossy-pleased, the pipe a monster rising from the waves without a head. I sit astride and let it inch me up the shore. A mighty quivering; a pause; another monumental shake. My mouth is moving, and I know I'm thinking that with this done I can pack my bags for home, for somewhere else. What I'm saying is quite different. I'm shouting something about Venus rising from the waves, the pipe my shell. Looking back, I see I meant Saint George – or any soldier, come to that, who'd

found a cause and knew the world would pay him, if he went
to war.

                    *

There used to be the pure wilderness of rock and sky;
now there is a game of scaffolding, and roads unravelling:
                    wherever next in the world,
                              and when?

There used to be tulips flashflooding the least of our valleys;
now there are gardens, and trim lawns balding at midday:
                    wherever next in the world,
                              and when?

There used to be tribes inching down hills with the snow;
now there are fences, and the locked gates of our camp:
                    wherever next in the world,
                              and when?

There used to be houses down backstreets with no address;
now there are maps, and torches swirled into my face:
                    wherever next in the world,
                              and when?

There used to be voices praying to fires burning in rock;
now there are drills whining, and typewriters in offices:
                    wherever next in the world,
                              and when?

There used to be me alone, hearing the bare sky sing;
now there is a car waiting, and suitcases piled in the hall:
                    wherever next in the world,
                              and when?

Four

The last time I fell to earth
was north again, colder, nearer the country of my birth.

You want to know exactly where?
All I can tell you is *there* and *there* and *there* and *there*.

You want to know exactly when?
Now and then I can tell you, *now and then*.

But let me be clear. I dispersed like a shower of rain
anywhere in the world you care to name,

anywhere, that is, as long as you remember I was still Joe,
the Joe everyone knows

and has read about, listened to, seen on TV
every time the earth changes its worn-out history

and frontiers break, seas boil, mountains explode,
people block what should be free-travelling roads,

and I am sent out to die in some shit-hole basement lair.
Don't say you don't know what I mean. You've seen me there.

*

I have been here for ever –
I won't name the town,
you take your pick –
in a basement-cave
one flight below ground
of a high-rise block.
with its eyes burnt out.

There's a pillar-box slit
high in one wall
so half each day
I can see into space:
smashed crests of tile,
and beyond them a ridge
of scrawny trees.

I don't need to look
to know what else:
quick rifle smoke
like a man who coughs
on a bitter morning;
the sapling lash
when artillery fires.

The last things you'll know
will be how I have lived,
and what I believed –
oh yes, and my name,
which I'd tell you now
if you didn't yet know
and I thought it would help.

Down here, you see,
the world has dissolved
and I cannot decide
what matters, what not.
I might once have said 'love'
when people could hear
and make something change.

Today I'll say 'food',
something simple like that —
food and the sense
that the turning earth
might wind itself back
then start once more
on a different course.

Ah, here's the sun now
posting in through its slit,
and another day stirs
with smoke on the hills.
I'm at home here, yes.
This is all I possess.
I am trying to live.

*

Then dark comes back with storms against the sun —
at least, I think it does: my pillar-box window's blank,
my basement-cave a vault of rancid air
where everything's made up except my life.

My life; my life. Above, among the streets
and market squares, I'd have to rack my brains
to float off anywhere outside myself.
Down here it's easy. I might not exist.

I see a flock of families on a beach somewhere.
They were my neighbours. Now they're dressed for snow
in overcoats and hats and prickly suits
but suffering in a silly press of heat.

Along the dunes behind them stands their stuff
or some of it – a flock of suitcases,
a bureau with a smashed-in top, a typewriter,
whatever they could carry when the whistle went.

They love each other, you can tell they do –
they have to, since they lost so much at once;
each other's lives are all that they've got left;
they are the past and everything ahead.

So when a boy breaks ranks and doodles off
to sit down weeping at the water's edge,
the last thing I expect is what comes next:
his mother narrowing her mouth, then crouched

and skating down the sand to pull him back,
whip off his hopeless cap (his father's size),
and thrash him for his sadness: *Don't you dare!*
I cannot hear the rest, but what I know, I know.

*

I had parents, but I don't remember.
I had a woman who loved me but she disappeared.
The streets
wherever I am
are all strange to me
with their ripped-up wiry roots,
and the parks all closed
although their beautifully wrought iron gates no longer shut.

I put these words down carefully side by side
like a child building a sentence –
parents, woman, streets, parks –
and they just lie there.
They never become a story.

Perhaps I have lived for too long.
You can do that, you know.
You can spend all your life thinking
More room! More room!
and *Not here but here!*
then one day learn a single minute
can hurt so much it lasts for ever.
That's when you wish everything over.

I mean:
think of the patient with gangrene
who has watched the disease munch its way up his leg
like a slug eating lettuce,
and knows it has finally worked right through.
Think of the young man taken out to be shot
who stands with his back to the gun
and his shoulders hunched
like a boy about to be slapped.
Both these know they have lived for too long.

On the other hand forget them
and think instead of the thunder
which is in fact the noise of hand-carts trundled by refugees.
They have piled up the words left to them
and are off somewhere, they don't know where,
to lay them out carefully side by side
and make their first sentence in a new language.

This is what I have done
watching the hand-carts trailing past my window-slit,
imagining the prayers said on the off-chance,
hearing the *slap, slap* of slippers on wet pavements,
the gunfire pausing then starting again.

One of my arms has been jolted off due west,
the other east,
my legs have been dispatched across different oceans.

Much more of this and I shall lose my head.
Then I will know for certain that I have lived too long.

In the meantime I shall stay put,
wherever I am,
no story left,
waiting for a miracle.

   *

A satellite-eye reports on the earth
     to a listening dish,
its silver messages filtering down:
     shoosh, shoosh.

Will it see me next? Will it see me?

It sees a dark stain in the mountains
    – disease in a lung –
then the camera whirrs into close-up and look
    the stain is a town.

What will it see next? What will it see?

It sees two dug-in lines of artillery firing
    either side of a river,
ant columns wriggling from house to house,
    and no bridge over.

Will it see me next? Will it see me?

It sees factory chimneys minus their heads
    a trench in a park,
sandbag castles turning the town hall yellow,
    a traffic jam of tanks.

What will it see next? What will it see?

It sees a minuscule dot among high-rise rubble
    which looks like a fire,
but might be the terrified, rolled back, rearing
    white of my eye.

Will it see me next? Will it see me?

*

Yes of course it's my eye,
my wriggling eye,
at its pillar-box slit
which squirms to escape
the world of things
and leap straight to the sun
like dew of a morning.

Look back? No point.
The hills of the past
heave out of each other
like waves in the wake
of a queasy yacht:
each one means another,
each death is the same.

Look forward? I can't.
My life still ahead
glares like the ice
some North Pole fool
thinks he can cross
on his wits alone:
of course he can't.

I'm trapped, you see,
trapped in the heart
of each glassy second:
I might be the hands
of a watch in their circle;
a fly in a jam jar
unhinging itself.

But it's worse than that.
Trapped with me here
(trapped in my head)
are the things I want not
to have seen in the world,
things I cannot tear out
behind my eyes:

the carpenter's son
some men took in half
with a well-loved saw
eventually;
a market garden
planted with heads;
that child's tongue;

the woman whose life
was wrenched to an O
too painful to speak.
Yes of course it's my eye
at its pillar-box slit,
my wriggling eye
which squirms to escape.

*

Let me tell you about the time before this,
when I could travel at will,
and a storm suddenly brewed up and boiled over,
drowning the sun.

It caught me half way over the local mountains
in a tired car,
and washed away whole loops of the road in red mud,
so I stopped at this café

– a whitewashed shack I'd noticed before but never entered –
and ordered a coke;
the owner, let's call him X, had his right hand missing
and wouldn't speak.

Cornered, I looked at the knobbly wall over his shoulder
and there was a photo
of men among rocks, swaddled with ammunition belts,
grinning like monkeys.

One of them was obviously X although it was years ago,
before his café days,
when the mountain road was only a zig-zag for goats,
and he still had his hand.

I might have wanted to hear his story and show pity
for all he knew,
but the one time our eyes met I knew it was wrong even
to ask for a second drink.

In fact he whisked my glass away before I'd quite finished
but I said nothing,
stepping out onto the drenched earth just as the sun
burnt back into place.

I saw near the car a stone cross I'd missed coming in.
It was covered with names –
codgers, boys, every age in between: all men, and all
killed the same day.

Across the road was another memorial, this one
a heraldic beast,
and something carved round the base in a language
no one here speaks.

X stood in his dark café, watching to make sure
.I bowed my head at the first.
Then he lifted his stump in some sort of salute to show
I could now drive away.

    *

You see, I have been above ground – and more
than once. At other times I have seen the builder
who crept out to stand patiently in a bread queue
and came home with both his legs blown off;
I have seen the doctor fucked by so many men
she must cry out her eyes for the rest of her life
and her children as well; I have seen the family
wheeling all they possess to a drab check-point
where one soldier, a boy really, turns them away
but keeps their grandfather clock and their money.

Yes I have seen all these things and brought them back
to my hole underground, my earth, my lair, my set,
where I have flicked through and through them
in the same way that I have also turned over the pages
of history books which have pointed out to me in the space
of a few moments how I might as well have been a refugee

a million times, or a red-faced soldier who was fired on
by the first tank ever, or a spy wearing a parachute,
or an executioner, or a patriot in the hills who has
what he has but leaves everyone else with nothing.

Yes I might have been any of these things and still
feel certain that not one of their lessons is learnt,
none of their patterns broken, their vocabularies lost,
even though we have started to run out of words ourselves
or letters at least (which means the words will follow)
as I saw with my own eyes on my last trip into the open
at the funeral of Anna, a girl who trod on a land mine
but is one of so many dead that when the time came
to hammer the letters of her name up on her cross
there were no As left, so now she is just -nn-, like that.

                  *

   O and one more thing:
from the rubble of a dead bungalow a father
wearing a blood-shadow on his jersey.
   Don't ask me how it got there.

   O and one more thing:
in the dawn smoke of a bare street a soldier
heaving a black plastic bag which still twitches.
   Don't ask me what is in there.

   O and one more thing:
beneath the skin of the harbour basin a wound
leaking pus which boils when it meets the surface.
   Don't ask me what goes on there.

    O and one more thing:
on the wind through the whole city a blizzard
of human cinders which are warm and taste sweet.
    Don't ask me how to live there.

    *

I let my face fall
from the window-slit;
now there's nothing to see
but the tree-covered hills
and the vulture sun
on a dangerous perch
rearranging its wings.

I recite the names
of my self and my home,
which cling to their map
with no more strength
than warm breath
on a window pane;
I breathe, I breathe.

I try to forget
the wounds I have heard
burst open and sob,
the tears I have watched
melt out of eyes
whose lids have gone
and can no longer sleep.

I do all these things
and feel I am tramping
through heart's blood
to reach a border
which someone has said
I have only to cross
to lose my life

and be given another.
The moment I get there
I stand to attention
and strain to discover
what lies ahead,
my hand to my brow
in a trembling salute.

But no, no,
there is nothing to see;
I have left the world
and come to the darkness
which surges through space,
the darkness which falls
when the very last star

has imploded and died,
and all that remains
are unliveable planets
hunting through nowhere,
rocking the air
with the hiss and rush
of their gas-cloud skirts.

Five

A country woman at the end of her life
might take a stroll round her mind's eye
and still see her villages for the first time:
Shutford, Radway, Hornton, Tysoe,
Alkerton, Oxhill, Sherington, Whatcote.

She might step out of her farmhouse early
catching the drift of every dew-soaked field
and still stand amazed with wonder:
Long Meadow, Burland, Drybank, Fant,
Heath, Middle, Hed, Stone Croft.

She might pat the fat flanks of a barn
hearing it has no room left to echo
and still know she can set others going:
Beggars, Bottle, Durnings, Tubs,
Magpie, Pleasure, Sweet Knowle, Bush.

She might crack the hard earth open
quarrying down past sand and gravel
and still enter the ground she most prizes:
Maidenhill, Puckpits, Rectory, Field,
St Dennis, Hum, Nardley Break, Holt.

She might stand on a stone bridge
between one place she knows and the next
and still feel she belongs to both:
Honington, Castle, Sotshole, Tithe,
Roundham, Valley, Ready, Newfoundland.

Our reference: Y3245

Warwickshire Constabulary
Shipston-upon-Stour Police Station
Stratford Road

Date: 4 January 1993

Report taken by: Green (D.I.)
On: Margaret Atkins (Miss)

Following a telephone call received by the Front Desk at 09.12 a.m. on 3 January, I investigated an incident at St Stephen's Farm, approximately five (5) miles north-east of Shipston-upon-Stour. The incident involved Miss Margaret Atkins, who was reported to be in a state of considerable distress, although no precise reason was given. Miss Atkins is ninety (90) years of age, and has spent all her life at St Stephen's Farm, which she inherited from her father Michael Atkins on his death in 1963.

Fifteen (15) years ago Miss Atkins suffered a stroke which impaired her speech and left her partially paralysed. Since that time the Department of Health and Social Security has repeatedly recommended a nurse. Miss Atkins has always denied that she needed help. The use of her left arm is restricted, and she is blind in her left eye. Although she is alone in her house she has arranged that her farm be run by a tenant, Mr John Smith (9 Heath Cottages, Shipston).

I arrived at St Stephen's Farm at 11.25 a.m. and proceeded to the front door. It is a stone farmhouse, but obviously delapidated. I rang the bell. There was no answer. After several more attempts I let myself in. The door was not locked.

The interior of the house is more severely run-down than the exterior. The floor of the main hall and all the downstairs and upstairs rooms are covered with newspapers, some of them many years old. Much of the furniture is broken or damaged. The electricity has been cut off. The windows are thickly coated with grime. The surfaces are dusty, and there is a strong smell of urine and faeces.

I discovered Miss Atkins upstairs in her bedroom. She was lying on, not in, the bed. She was wearing a nightdress and no other garment, even though the temperature was only a little above freezing. The disorganization of the upper part of the house was even worse than the lower. Miss Atkins was fully conscious but spoke with difficulty.

I immediately covered Miss Atkins with a blanket and telephoned for an ambulance. Whilst waiting for this to arrive, Miss Atkins informed me that she had not asked to be taken from her home. She said that she had telephoned the Station because she had something to tell the police. She said that she believed she was nearing the end of her life and wanted to confess to a crime. I indulged her in this. Miss Atkins told me that her brother, Captain Thomas (T. A.) Atkins, who is presumed to have died in a shooting accident at St Stephen's Farm many years previously, was in fact killed deliberately.

I advised Miss Atkins that she should not distress herself, but she became increasingly agitated. She had no detail to substantiate her story. She recommended that I look up the case in our files at the Station. (I have since done this: see below.) She had some newspaper clippings of her own dated January 1918, which she instructed me to find in a cupboard by her bedside. This I did. While I was perusing them the ambulance arrived (at 12.02 p.m.), and Miss Atkins was taken to Shipston Cottage Hospital. Mr John Smith, her manager, has been informed, and so has the Department of Health and Social Security (reference PT502).

I understood Miss Atkins's allegations to be a result of her confused state of mind. On returning to the Station, however, I examined the files relating to the case she had mentioned: namely, that of her brother Captain T. A. Atkins, who was killed in a shooting accident on 3 January 1918 (reference B2715; 4/1/18). It appears that he slipped on wet grass while shooting rabbits, and accidentally discharged his gun. The only witeness to the death was a Captain Joseph Soap of the Manchester Regiment, who was listed as 'missing presumed killed' in France later that year. I find nothing doubtful about the evidence presented to the inquest at the time, and see no reason to re-open the case. All those involved, with the exception of Miss Atkins herself, are dead. There are no suspicious circumstances.

Signed

Green (D. I.)

*

I planted my love in the ground,
Not in the heart of a man —
I knew a man would turn on me
And scare me with his gun.

O yes, I've seen it happen —
It even happens out here,
In these lonely acres no one knows
And innocent-looking air.

Wings burst out of a treetop,
The silky barrels rise,
And something that's neither bird nor beast
Slithers down the skies.

Or a rabbit pops out of a hedgerow,
Tentative, ears alive,
And a single explosion murders me
And everything I love.

You think I'm speaking in riddles?
I don't care if you do.
You'll never believe what I have seen,
But I know what is true.

*

From the *Birmingham Post*, 3 February 1993

CHARACTER DIES
By a Staff Reporter

Local residents were today saddened to learn of the death of Miss Margaret Atkins, aged ninety. For thirty years, Miss Atkins had farmed at St Stephen's, Shipston-upon-Stour, where she was born. Neighbours were accustomed to see her riding in the surrounding area wearing fashions from long ago. She refused to move with the times and acquired a reputation as 'a character'. Police, who were summoned to the farm a month ago when she first became ill, described her state of mind as 'confused'.

St Stephen's will shortly be sold at auction. Browns of Shipston will be handling the sale.

*

Although Margaret would have liked to sit up listening to Joe and her brother Tom, and knew their leave would soon be over, her concentration started to go at ten, and she was upstairs asleep by eleven. At midnight she was woken by creaking and clumping overhead. It was Joe; his bedroom was directly above her own. She went back to sleep again, but an hour later the same thing happened. And again an hour after that. She debated whether to go up to him and complain, but decided not to. She couldn't blame Joe. It wasn't until five that the noises stopped and she finally fell asleep. When dawn broke, and she should have been laying fires and sorting out the breakfast things, she was still dead to the world. Never mind, said her father as he cleared the table. Leave her. She's only young.

He suggested that Tom and Joe went ferreting for rabbits. He would like to come with them and take a turn himself, but he'd better not. There was plenty else for him to do around the farm, and what with no help this year – well, he'd rather see the boys go alone.

Without looking at Tom, Joe immediately said yes, he would like that. Mr Atkins clapped his hands and led the way to the back door, where they all began pulling on boots and overcoats. Margaret appeared, crumpled and sheepish. Where were they going, she asked. Staunchill Ditch. Could she come with them. No, said Joe. She was surprised to hear him so stern, and frowned; she hadn't been asking him anyway, she'd been asking Tom. Her father put his hand on her arm and whispered something that sounded like: You'll be snoring. She realized it must have been: It's their last morning. Then he ushered the boys outside into the yard and pulled the door behind him. It didn't shut tight. As it swung slowly open again it showed Margaret still in the dark passage, watching them.

In the stables, Mr Atkins slipped the two ferrets out of their cage. They were pure white with virulently pink eyes. When Mr Atkins held them over the open sack for a moment, gripping them by the scruff of their necks, they squeaked, opening their mouths and showing yellow teeth. There was something obsequious about them, with their plaintive noises and their dangling forepaws.

Slow down, there's no rush, Tom wanted to say as he and Joe set off along the track which would bring them to the Ditch. The rain of the last few days had made the mud slippery, but it was hard underneath; there was still frost in it. Joe cleared his throat to speak, then just shrugged.

As she kept her distance behind them, Margaret thought they were a picture of good companions. She could appreciate, now, why Joe had told her to stay behind. She still wanted to watch them, though. Joe looked so intent as he bent forward cradling the gun, the hem of his big green coat snapping against his legs. Tom had the sack with the ferrets in it slung over his back.

When they reached Staunchill Ditch, Margaret fell further behind, then left the track altogether and tucked herself into the lea of a hawthorn hedge. She crouched down. The boys would probably see her on their way home, but it wouldn't matter so much then.

She saw Joe hand the gun to her brother, then take hold of the sack. There was something solemn about the exchange, with the figures silent and the wide grey sky behind them, but also something absurd. They were only two boys shooting rabbits. There was nothing more to it. Joe turned quickly away and strode towards the Ditch, jumping across it then dragging the brambles away from the rabbit holes and sliding the ferrets out of their sack.

If the boys spoke to each other after that, Margaret couldn't hear what they were saying. The wind drowned them. They were too far off. Joe stayed kneeling on the bank, occasionally pressing the side of his face to the earth – he was listening for the ferrets underground – and once or twice sliding his arm into a hole.

Tom slouched with his gun in the open. For a minute there was nothing – then a rabbit bounced out of the earth beside Joe and into the field. Tom jerked to attention, lifting the gun and swinging in an arc which followed the rabbit. He fired once. The recoil of the shot kicked him in the shoulder, making him stagger, and a miniature cloud emerged from the muzzle.

Tom let the rabbit lie. This took Margaret aback. She had expected him to collect it, to leave the field tidy and admire what he had killed. But of course he had shot rabbits a thousand times before. There was nothing new in it for him. Her surprise turned to boredom and she wished she had stayed back at the farm. She was hungry. The wind blew steadily colder. But if she left now the boys would certainly see her. They would think less of her. She settled further into the hedge, resting her weight on her heels, hugging her knees.

Suddenly Tom was running. She couldn't understand why – nothing had changed. Joe was still kneeling on the far side of the Ditch. The ferrets were still underground. She heard Tom shouting but couldn't make out the words. Two rabbits spurted towards him simultaneously, side by side, then divided round him so that he turned a full half-circle and shot after them, using both barrels but missing. He reloaded and seemed to be laughing; he had unbuttoned his coat and it ballooned round him as he ran. Then Joe shouted something and Tom stopped running. He must have been excited, Margaret thought, that's all. Two, three, four more rabbits bobbed towards him and he raised his gun again. This time he killed one perfectly, the shot striking full-face, solid as an iron bar, so the rabbit turned head over heels.

Joe stood up, brushed his knees, and jumped back into the field. Obviously he was going to swap places with Tom. He walked with the same elongated, business-like stride she had noticed before. She saw Tom offer the gun to his friend. He was holding it longways in both hands like a peace-offering, and she imagined them smiling at each other. Just a few more minutes, they were saying. A few more shots, then they would hoik out the ferrets and try again somewhere else.

But they weren't smiling. Joe seemed to be tugging at the gun, and Tom was pulling it back away from him. Not pulling. Heaving. Was it a game? Margaret could see their mouths opening and closing but the wind took whatever they said. She wanted to be at home and know nothing about this. At the same time, she wanted to be closer and understand it. She held her breath for so long that her ears started to ring.

Everything came closer. The gun rocked to and fro between the boys like a log in water, but there was never any doubt that Joe would finally win it. Or not win it, exactly. Control it. Swivel it round so the butt was pointing towards the ground and the muzzle was jammed underneath Tom's chin. As soon as it was arranged like that, fixed straight up between heaven and earth, Tom's head flung backwards. A little jagged thing like an antler stuck out of his forehead. The antler flopped down, useless. Tom flopped down. Joe lunged as if to catch him by the coat, and as he did this the bang of the shot at last rolled over Margaret. Joe fumbled at the body but couldn't stop it falling. Tom ended up face down, the gun hidden beneath him. Margaret started to breathe again and the cold wind came back, crackling the hedge, blowing straight through her.

There was no chance of escaping now. When Joe started back to the farm he would see her; he was bound to. As soon as he had collected the ferrets he would turn round and there she would be. He had scrambled across the ditch and was lying on the ground by the rabbit holes again, one long arm underground. It was difficult, retrieving ferrets, Margaret knew that, but it would only take five minutes. That was all she had. No. Not even five minutes. Joe had found both creatures; he was already tying up the neck of the sack. He must have kept the piece of twine her father had used in the stables. He must have wound it into a ball and pushed it into the pocket of his overcoat. He was a tidy man. A methodical man. He did not look down at Tom as he leapt back into the field and began walking towards her, moving with his strong insistent strides.

Margaret stood up straight to meet him. She knew he would not hurt her. He had no reason to do that. There had only been one thing for him to do, and he had done it. She understood this, but still wanted to hear Joe explaining everything. She wanted him to tell her, so that he would be able to see she had made her choice, and would keep his secret.

He neither broke his stride, nor coloured, nor looked round to see whether anyone else was with her. He loomed right up to her and stopped, looking down at her, as close as he had stood to Tom. He was a little out of breath and there was a smear of blood on his chin where he had nicked himself shaving. Margaret felt the heat coming off his body in the loose green coat.

Joe spoke in short sentences, never raising his voice, making everything simple. He said it was because of the war. He, Joe, knew what war was like. He had seen it, remember. He had seen everything there was to see. He knew that he had managed to stay alive only by accident. But he would not survive when he went back this time. It would be impossible. And it would have been the same for Tom. Tom would not have survived either, and before he died he would have been frightened, ashamed, mutilated, driven out of his mind. It was better for him to die here, at home. This was certain. He was not making anything up.

Margaret nodded; she told him she understood.

Joe said he must go back to the farm and find her father, and say what had happened. Was there a hand-cart somewhere on which they could carry the body? Yes, there was. Margaret told him she would find her own way back to the farm. Joe said they would see each other again later in the day, even though he was going to be busy now, there was a lot to do, and soon he would be gone.

*

I spent my time in the light and all weathers
even though it was death I knew best and loved most.

    I am here in the world
    broken apart
    alone and apart,
    never again as myself.

I locked and bolted my door far off from anyone else
even though I had all the ways of the world by heart.

    I can fall to the ground
    one piece at a time
    any moment in time,
    never again as myself.

I buried myself deep down in the ground and was saved
even though I saw nothing and learnt what it means to be lost.

I can come back and live
whenever I like
as whatever I like,
never again as myself.

I kept my promise of silence each day of my life
even though I have raised the dead and called them my own.

I can speak in my voice
in a hundred tongues
without moving my tongue,
never again as myself.